A robot timeline

420 BC

The Greek mathematician Archytas of Tarentum builds a wooden bird that can flap its wings.

17th–18th centuries

Inventors make mechanical people and animals, called automatons, that can move, play musical instruments, draw pictures and write.

1994

Dante II, a robot with eight legs, explores a volcano crater.

AD 1495

Leonardo da Vinci designs a mechanical knight in armour, a humanoid robot.

1954

The first modern industrial robots are developed.

1981

The Space Shuttle Orbiter is equipped with a robot arm for picking up and moving equipment in space.

1999

Sony makes a robot toy in the form of a dog called AIBO.

2001

A robot spy-plane called a Global Hawk flies itself 13,000 kilometres (8,000 miles) from California to Australia.

2013

The US space agency, NASA, builds a robot called GROVER, designed to explore the Arctic ice sheets while measuring the thickness of the ice.

1996

Honda builds the P2 (Prototype 2) robot that can walk, climb stairs and carry things.

2000

Honda builds the most advanced humanoid robot to date, a small figure called ASIMO.

2004

Engineers at Cornell University in the USA build a robot helicopter just 7 centimetres (3 inches) tall.

What is a robot?

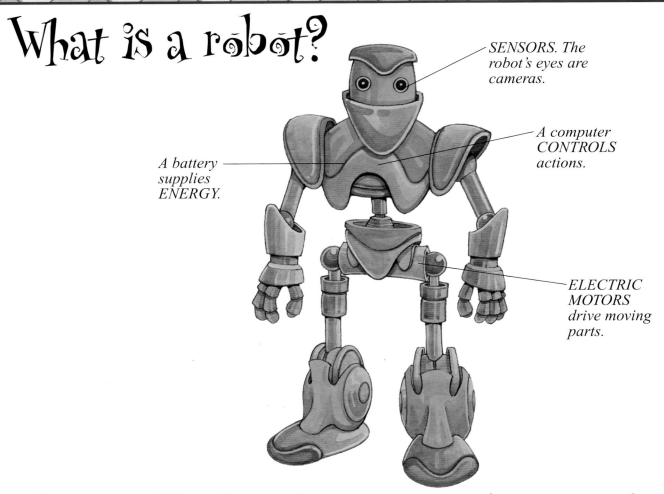

SENSORS. The robot's eyes are cameras.

A computer CONTROLS actions.

A battery supplies ENERGY.

ELECTRIC MOTORS drive moving parts.

Robots are machines that can be programmed to carry out a series of complex actions automatically or under the control of an operator. They come in all shapes and sizes, from mechanical arms and driverless vehicles to walking, talking, artificial people. Whatever they look like and however big or small they are, all robots have the same four features –

sensors, motion, energy and control. Sensors can collect lots of information from the robot's surroundings. A motion system moves the different parts of the robot, usually by means of electric motors. The energy needed to make it work is, in most cases, electricity supplied by batteries. The robot is controlled either by a computer or a human operator.

Author:

Ian Graham earned a degree in applied physics at City University, London. He then earned a graduate diploma in journalism. Since becoming a freelance author and journalist, he has written more than 250 children's nonfiction books.

Artist:

David Antram was born in Brighton, England, in 1958. He studied at Eastbourne College of Art and then worked in advertising for 15 years before becoming a full-time artist. He has illustrated many children's non-fiction books.

Series creator:

David Salariya was born in Dundee, Scotland. He has illustrated a wide range of books and has created and designed many new series for publishers in the UK and overseas. David established The Salariya Book Company in 1989. He lives in Brighton with his wife, illustrator Shirley Willis, and their son, Jonathan.

Editor: Jonathan Ingoldby

Editorial Assistant: Mark Williams

Published in Great Britain in MMXIX by
Book House, an imprint of
The Salariya Book Company Ltd
25 Marlborough Place, Brighton BN1 1UB
www.salariya.com

ISBN: 978-1-912537-06-8

1 3 5 7 9 8 6 4 2

A CIP catalogue record for this book is available from the British Library.
Printed and bound in China.

Visit
www.salariya.com
for our online catalogue and
free fun stuff.

PAPER FROM
SUSTAINABLE
FORESTS

You Wouldn't Want to Live Without™

Robots!

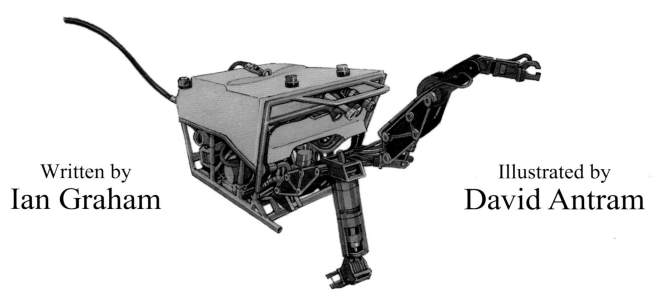

Written by
Ian Graham

Illustrated by
David Antram

Series created by
David Salariya

BOOK HOUSE
a SALARIYA *imprint*

Contents

Introduction

If you think robots are future technology or movie trickery, think again. Real robots are here now. Millions of them already work in factories, hospitals and homes. There are robots in space too, helping astronauts and exploring the solar system. Some work with people, or in place of people. Imagine a world without robots. If they weren't here, some of the jobs we do might be much harder, and many of the jobs they do, some dangerous or in difficult locations or environments, might have to be done by people. So, you really wouldn't want to live in a world without robots.

REPETITIVE WORK

VARIED WORK

9

What's so good about robots?

Lots of the things you use every day were built with the help of robots. Robots are used because they often perform better than people. Robots can work round the clock without having to take breaks or go home. They don't get tired. They don't need holidays or fall ill. And they can work faster and more accurately than people. What do you think would happen if robots weren't here? If people had to replace them, complex products like computers and cars would take longer to build and they would probably cost more.

POWERFUL ROBOTS are far stronger than human workers. They can move amazingly heavy things around easily and with pinpoint precision.

Harrumph... weakling!

Hope it's not me they're looking for...

SOME ROBOTS WORK TOGETHER in teams or swarms, like bees or ants. Swarm robots are being developed for search and rescue work, and also for military operations.

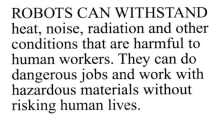

Wow! That's too hot for me!

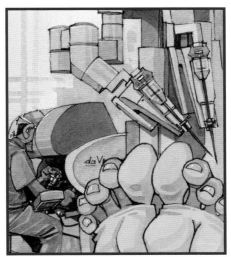

ROBOTS CAN WITHSTAND heat, noise, radiation and other conditions that are harmful to human workers. They can do dangerous jobs and work with hazardous materials without risking human lives.

DA VINCI is a robotic surgery system. It performs surgery on patients under the control of a surgeon. The robot changes the surgeon's hand movements into smaller, steadier movements of the instruments.

ROBOTS COMPETE against each other in all sorts of activities. Every year teams of robots take part in an international football competition called the RoboCup.

How old are robots?

Robots have been here for a lot longer than you might think. There were robots in the ancient world, more than 2,000 years ago. They weren't called robots, because the word *robot* hadn't been invented yet. They were known as automata, which means 'automatic machines'. There were no computers, batteries or electric motors, so automata were simpler than modern robots. They couldn't be programmed to do different things. They were often built to look like animals, with moving legs or wings. Some were built to look like living people and were able to write, draw or play a musical instrument.

LEONARDO'S KNIGHT. In 1495 the famous Italian artist, engineer and inventor Leonardo da Vinci designed a robot knight in armour. If it had been built, it could have stood up, sat down, moved its arms and raised its visor.

I was way ahead of my time.

THE DIGESTING DUCK. In 1738, a French inventor, Jacques de Vaucanson, made a life-size robot duck. It ate grain and produced poo!

Hmm... not one of my best ideas.

Some early robots were driven by water power or steam, but most were powered by wind-up clockwork motors, using the energy stored in a spring.

THE TURK. An automaton called the Turk was built in the late 1700s. The figure played chess and often defeated good chess players. Its secret was an operator hidden inside its desk.

KARAKURI. Automata called *karakuri* were popular in Japan in the 18th and 19th centuries. They performed on stage and in religious ceremonies. Small karakuri puppets were also used to serve cups of tea.

13

Industrial robots

Businesses are always keen to use new materials, methods and machines to cut their costs and make better products. They were quick to start using robots. Today, there are more than a million industrial robots at work all over the world. Factories use them to make all sorts of things. Without their fast, precise and high-quality work, lots of products would cost more and they probably wouldn't be quite as well made or as reliable as they are. However, robots have replaced large numbers of human workers, who have had to find other types of work to do, and in some cases be trained in new skills.

THE FIRST INDUSTRIAL ROBOT was a mechanical arm called Unimate. In 1961, it started work in a car factory in New Jersey, USA, doing the dangerous job of unloading hot metal parts from a casting machine.

Wow! Rather you than me!

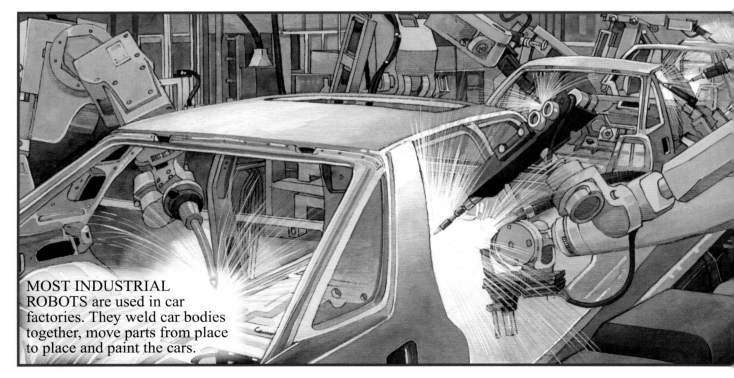

MOST INDUSTRIAL ROBOTS are used in car factories. They weld car bodies together, move parts from place to place and paint the cars.

ROBOTS WHIZZ AROUND warehouses at up to 50 kilometres per hour (30 miles per hour) storing goods on the shelves. When the goods are needed, the robots know where they are and fetch them just as fast.

Stop showing off!

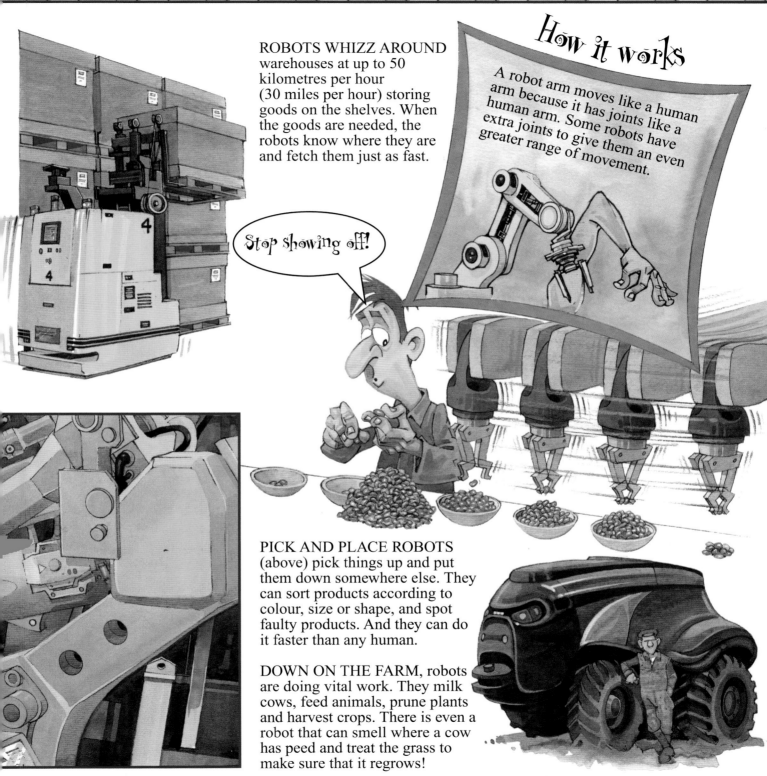

How it works

A robot arm moves like a human arm because it has joints like a human arm. Some robots have extra joints to give them an even greater range of movement.

PICK AND PLACE ROBOTS (above) pick things up and put them down somewhere else. They can sort products according to colour, size or shape, and spot faulty products. And they can do it faster than any human.

DOWN ON THE FARM, robots are doing vital work. They milk cows, feed animals, prune plants and harvest crops. There is even a robot that can smell where a cow has peed and treat the grass to make sure that it regrows!

15

Travel and transport

Robots are better, safer drivers than people. They aren't distracted by passengers talking to them. They don't get tired and, with the help of satellite navigation, they don't get lost. The numbers of robot vehicles are growing all the time. There are already driverless trains and robot planes, and the first driverless cars are now being tested on public roads. In the future, car owners might not need to know how to drive! Robots will do it for them. Robotic vehicles of all sorts will be commonplace and we'll wonder how we ever managed without them.

THIS ROBOT PLANE, called a Global Hawk, is the size of a small airliner. It flew itself more than 13,000 kilometres (8,000 miles) from California, USA, all the way to Australia.

Laser maps surroundings

DRIVERLESS CARS are robots on wheels. They automatically find their own way, while keeping a safe distance from nearby vehicles and other obstacles.

Video camera detects objects

Radar measures distances

Wheel sensors monitor vehicle motion

Robot cars and other vehicles know exactly where they are because they receive radio signals from a fleet of satellites in orbit around the Earth. The satellites belong to the Global Positioning System (GPS).

I'd have no one to nag!

THESE TRUCKS IN AN AUSTRALIAN MINE have no-one in the driver's cab. The giant trucks are controlled from an office 1,600 kilometres (nearly 1,000 miles) away from the mine.

BIGDOG IS A WALKING ROBOT with four legs. It carries heavy loads like a pack mule. Having legs instead of wheels means that it can go wherever people can go on foot.

Walkies!

BD51 SMR

17

Helpers at home

Robots are beginning to appear in homes. There are robots to do the vacuum cleaning, robots to wash floors, robots to mow the lawn and even robots to play with. People who are ill, very old or live alone are sometimes unhappy or lonely. There are now robots designed to keep them company, like a robot pet. As new, smarter robots are developed, they will be able to do more jobs in the home. Household robots could become as common as washing machines are today, and just as hard to do without.

PARO IS A ROBOT SEAL designed to be a friend or pet for people in hospitals, care homes and their own homes. It moves, makes sounds and responds as if it enjoys being stroked.

The motors that make robots move are connected to electric circuits. You can make a simple electric circuit. Connect a 1.5-volt torch battery and bulb together with electrical connecting wire as shown. Electricity flows around the circuit and lights the bulb.

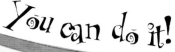

ROBOT TOYS are programmed to walk, play and even dance. Some of them can obey voice commands. There are robot dogs and dinosaurs, and human-shaped robots too.

ROBOT VACUUM CLEANERS criss-cross a room, brushing up dust and dirt. When they bump into something, they turn and go in another direction until the whole floor has been cleaned.

THE LATEST ROBOT HELPERS are smart enough to move around a home and avoid furniture while fetching and carrying things.

Buzz off!

19

Danger!

Robots help to keep human workers safe by doing the jobs that are too difficult or hazardous for people. One of the most dangerous jobs is mining. Some mines now use robot mining machines underground and robot trucks above ground. Robots have also been used to explore dangerous active volcanoes, and they have helped to clean up radioactive wreckage left by accidents in nuclear power stations. If these hazardous jobs couldn't be done by robots, they would have to be done by people, or they might not be done at all.

WHEN A NUCLEAR POWER STATION in Japan was damaged in 2011, the building was too radioactive to enter. Robots inspected the damage and helped with the clean-up.

ROBOTIC MINING MACHINES including rock cutters, drilling machines and diggers called LHDs (load, haul, dump machines) are used in underground mines.

Many of these robots are controlled by a person standing nearby with a control box. Moving the controls sends radio signals to the robot to steer it and operate its tools.

A WALKING ROBOT CALLED DANTE II (above) explored the crater of an active volcano in Alaska. It analysed poisonous gases pouring out of the crater.

SMALL ROBOTS do the highly dangerous job of checking suspicious vehicles and packages that might contain bombs. They are fitted with an arm carrying cameras, lights and mechanical hands called grippers.

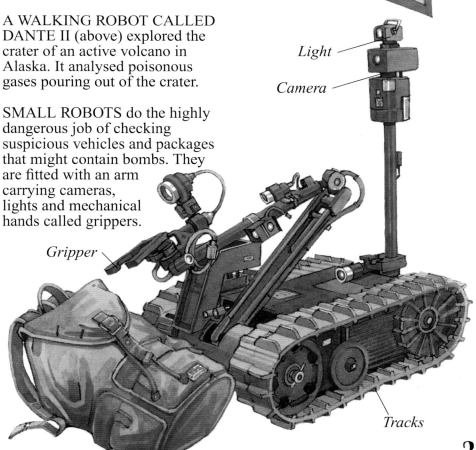

Light

Camera

Gripper

Tracks

21

Below the waves

The oceans are difficult to explore and work in. Most human divers cannot go deeper than about 30 metres (100 feet). Professionals can go deeper by using special equipment, but the deepest dives are made by robots. Most of them are remotely operated vehicles (ROVs) controlled by people on the surface, but there are also robots smart enough to dive completely under their own control. They're called autonomous underwater vehicles (AUVs). If there were no underwater robots, some of the deep-sea work done by industry would be impossible and scientists would know a lot less about the oceans.

He's up to no good!

THIS UNDERWATER ROBOT has been developed to explore deep coral reefs. It is designed to replace humans on dangerous dives.

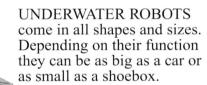

UNDERWATER ROBOTS come in all shapes and sizes. Depending on their function they can be as big as a car or as small as a shoebox.

LOST WRECKS of famous ships have been found by using underwater robots to search the seabed. Without robots, these shipwrecks might never have been found.

How it works

Vertical thruster

Horizontal thruster

Most underwater robots are equipped with lights, cameras, robot arms and battery-powered propellers called thrusters. The thrusters enable the robot to make very precise movements.

NEREUS (below) (lost at sea, 2014) was an underwater robot that could either be controlled from the surface or operate on its own. It could dive to the deepest parts of the oceans, 11,000 metres (36,000 feet) below the surface.

WITHOUT UNDERWATER ROBOTS, a lot of the vital work of inspecting and repairing deep-sea structures and pipelines would be very difficult or impossible to do.

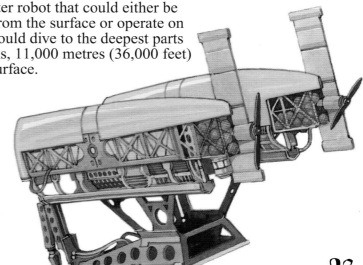

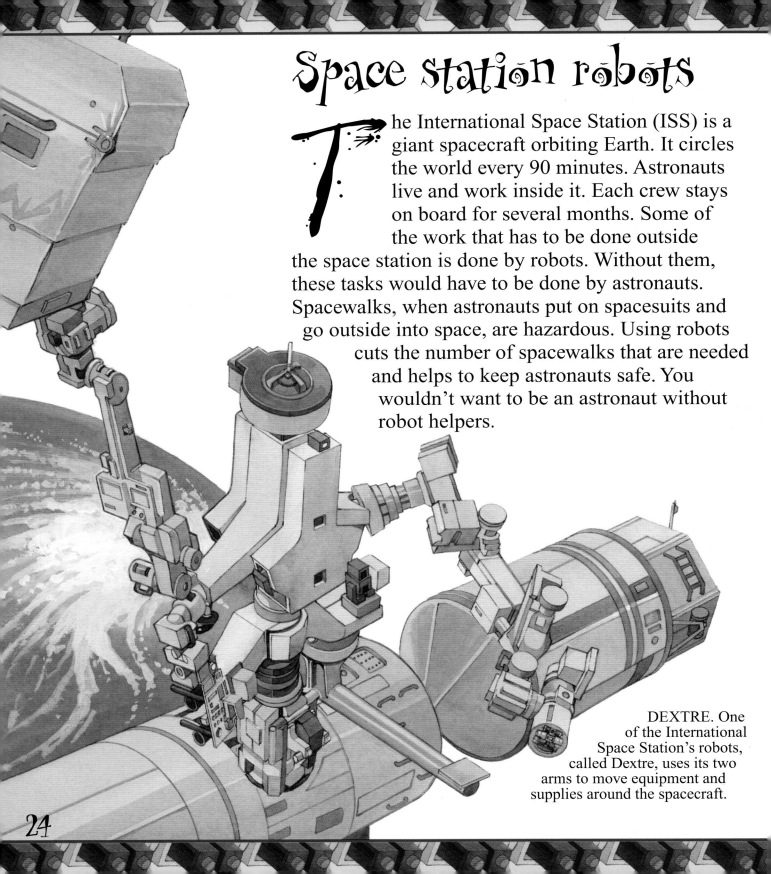

Space station robots

The International Space Station (ISS) is a giant spacecraft orbiting Earth. It circles the world every 90 minutes. Astronauts live and work inside it. Each crew stays on board for several months. Some of the work that has to be done outside the space station is done by robots. Without them, these tasks would have to be done by astronauts. Spacewalks, when astronauts put on spacesuits and go outside into space, are hazardous. Using robots cuts the number of spacewalks that are needed and helps to keep astronauts safe. You wouldn't want to be an astronaut without robot helpers.

DEXTRE. One of the International Space Station's robots, called Dextre, uses its two arms to move equipment and supplies around the spacecraft.

The robots that work outside the International Space Station are controlled by astronauts inside the station by using joysticks like games controllers. The robots can also be operated from Earth.

ROBOT ARM. The most massive loads, including new parts for the space station, are moved around by a robot arm called the remote manipulator system (RMS).

Hi, nice to meet you.

KIROBO. When Japanese astronaut Koichi Wakata arrived at the International Space Station in 2013, a tiny robot astronaut called Kirobo was there to welcome him on board.

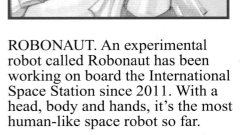

ROBONAUT. An experimental robot called Robonaut has been working on board the International Space Station since 2011. With a head, body and hands, it's the most human-like space robot so far.

Exploring the solar system

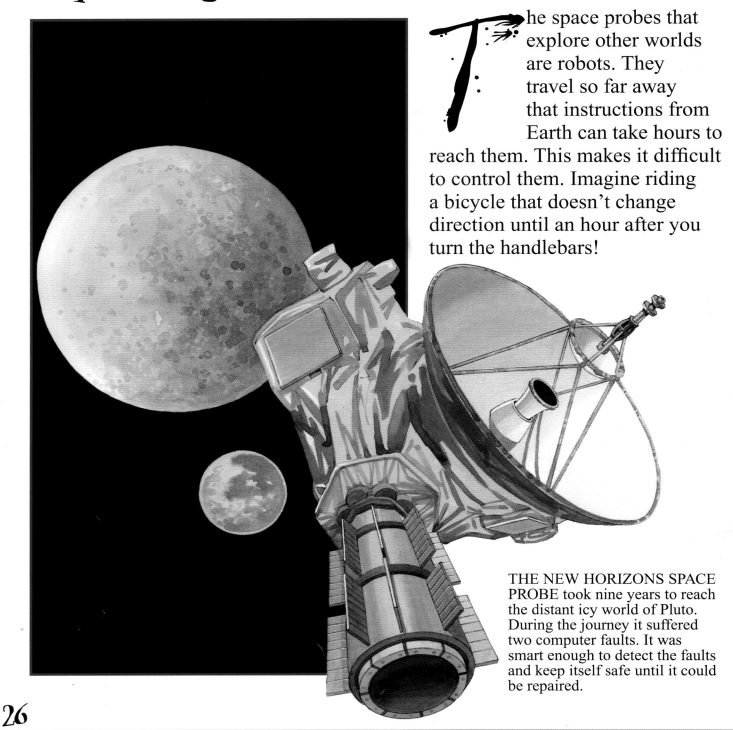

The space probes that explore other worlds are robots. They travel so far away that instructions from Earth can take hours to reach them. This makes it difficult to control them. Imagine riding a bicycle that doesn't change direction until an hour after you turn the handlebars!

THE NEW HORIZONS SPACE PROBE took nine years to reach the distant icy world of Pluto. During the journey it suffered two computer faults. It was smart enough to detect the faults and keep itself safe until it could be repaired.

Space probes have to be smart enough to deal with problems until controllers on Earth can help them. They usually keep themselves safe by shutting down faulty systems. If these smart probes didn't exist, we wouldn't know much about other planets, and we'd miss out on the awesome photographs taken by the probes.

How it works

Most robot spacecraft are in space for years. One way to power them is to make electricity from sunlight. Solar panels take in sunlight and change it into electric current.

NASA's JUNO SPACE PROBE (right) spotted a problem as it orbited Jupiter. It shut down all but its most important systems to protect itself while it waited for help from Earth.

A ROVER CALLED CURIOSITY landed on Mars in 2012. It is driven by people on Earth, but it is smart enough to spot dangers ahead and work out how to avoid them.

Androids

If robots and people are going to work together, sharing the same workplaces, robots will have to use the same tools, doorways, workbenches and equipment that people use, and do it safely. The best shape and size for a robot to do this is the human form. Robots that look like humans are called humanoids or androids. It has proved difficult to create a walking, talking, intelligent android – until now. There are now some very lifelike and smart androids. ASIMO is one of the most advanced humanoid robots. Standing 1.3 metres (4 feet 3 inches) tall, it can walk, climb stairs, recognise faces and gestures, understand voice commands and answer questions.

IT MAY NOT be long before you find yourself working alongside one. There might even be android teachers some day!

MIIM is a walking, talking humanoid robot. Its body is controlled by 30 electric motors. Another eight motors give it lifelike facial expressions.

Oh no – not TOPIO!

TOPIO is a cool-looking humanoid robot designed to play table tennis against human opponents. It uses artificial intelligence to learn and improve its game.

ROBOT RESEARCHERS are trying to create a lifelike robot face that can smile, frown and create all the other facial expressions that we humans use to communicate with each other.

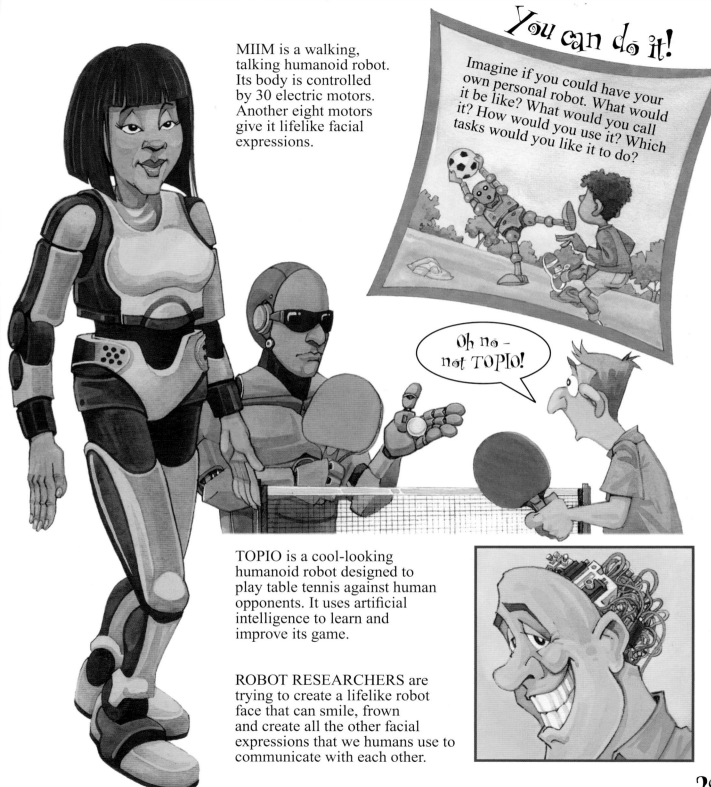

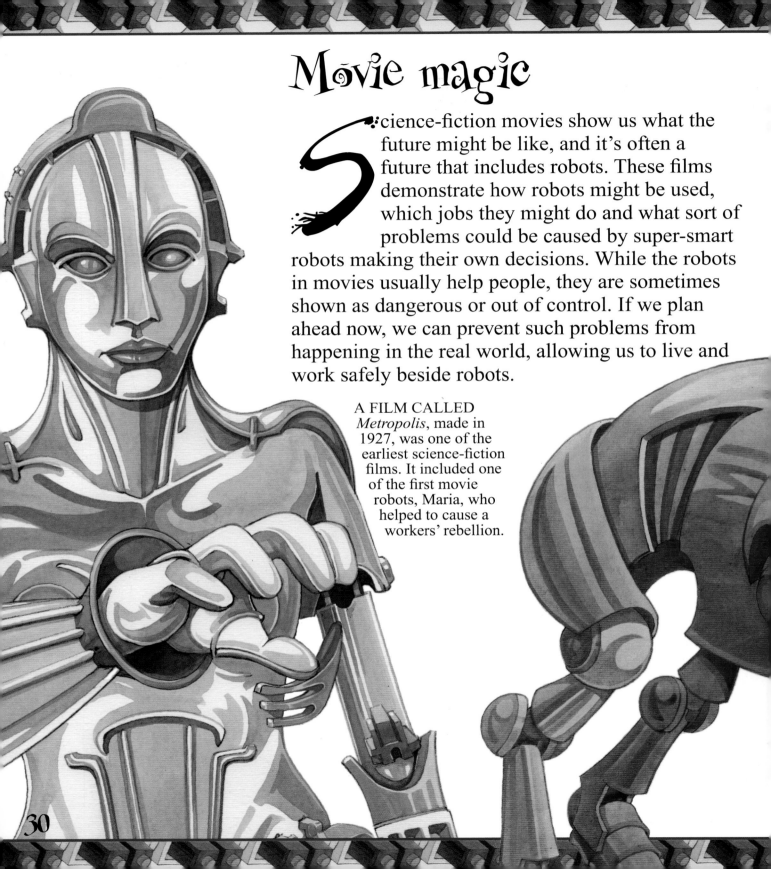

Movie magic

Science-fiction movies show us what the future might be like, and it's often a future that includes robots. These films demonstrate how robots might be used, which jobs they might do and what sort of problems could be caused by super-smart robots making their own decisions. While the robots in movies usually help people, they are sometimes shown as dangerous or out of control. If we plan ahead now, we can prevent such problems from happening in the real world, allowing us to live and work safely beside robots.

A FILM CALLED *Metropolis*, made in 1927, was one of the earliest science-fiction films. It included one of the first movie robots, Maria, who helped to cause a workers' rebellion.

ROBBY THE ROBOT starred in a film called *Forbidden Planet* in 1956. Robby was so popular that he, as well as the other robots based on him, starred in many other films and television programmes.

You can do it!

Make a list of robots from films and television programmes. How many of them are good robots and how many of them are bad? Which one is your favourite?

I had the strangest dream!

KILLER ROBOTS often appear in science-fiction films. Some of them were designed to be killers. Others turned into killers because of a fault, or perhaps hacking changed their behaviour.

SOME FILM ROBOTS claim to have feelings and even to have dreams. Could it be true? Do you think robots will always be just machines, or could they have feelings and dreams like us?

31

Do robots think?

If you think robots are intelligent today, the next generation will be even more so. The most advanced robots can already learn new skills without having to be programmed for them. If robots can learn like humans, will they think like humans? Could they even know that they exist in the same way that we do? Some scientists think this is possible. As robots become smarter, and do more complicated jobs, future generations of people may lose the skills they need to do the same jobs, making it harder for them to live without robots.

IN AN EXPERIMENT with three robots in New York in 2015, one of them appeared to show signs of self-awareness – it seemed to know that it existed!

ICUB IS A ROBOT being used by dozens of laboratories for artificial intelligence research. The size of a 3-year-old child, iCub can see, hear, touch and learn like a child.

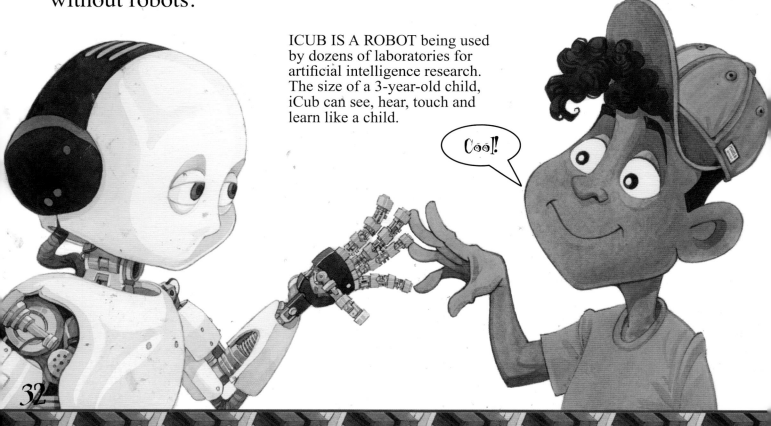

Cool!

32

Top tip

Be nice to your robot. You really don't want to upset it or make it angry. If it is really intelligent, do you think it would let you turn it off?

Don't even think about it!

IF AN INTELLIGENT ROBOT causes a road accident, who is to blame? Is it the fault of the robot, or the company that built it, or the people who programmed it?

IF FUTURE ROBOTS are able to think like humans and solve complex problems, would it be possible for a robot president to run a country?

Glossary

Android A robot that looks and moves like a human being.

Artificial intelligence The programming of a robot or other machine that enables it to learn and behave like a human being.

Automaton A mechanical figure or animal that moves automatically in a lifelike way under its own power.

Autonomous underwater vehicle (AUV) A robot designed to carry out tasks underwater automatically, without having to be controlled by a human operator.

Casting machine An industrial machine that makes metal parts by pouring molten metal into a mould.

Gripper Part of a robot that can close in order to grip or hold something, like a simple hand.

Hacking Breaking into a computer system to look at, or steal, data.

Hazardous Risky or dangerous.

Humanoid A robot that looks like a human being.

Industrial To do with industry (processing raw materials and manufacturing goods).

International Space Station (ISS) A giant spacecraft the size of a football field in orbit around Earth, operated by astronauts who live and work inside it for several months at a time.

Laser A device that produces an intense beam of pure light.

Navigation Planning a route from one place to another.

Nuclear power station A building where electricity is produced by a nuclear reactor, a device that makes use of the natural break-up of large particles of matter to release energy that is then used to heat water and make steam to drive generators.

Orbiter A spacecraft that orbits Earth or another world.

Pack mule A mule (the offspring of a male donkey and a female horse) that is used to carry heavy loads.

Program A set of instructions that tell a computer or robot what to do.

Prototype The first version of a device, machine, vehicle or system, built to test it and reveal any design faults.

Radar A device that detects objects in the distance by sending out bursts of radio waves and listening for any that bounce back from objects such as ships and aircraft.

Remotely operated vehicle (ROV) A mobile machine that is steered and controlled by someone from a distance.

Robonaut A humanoid robot astronaut developed to help human astronauts on board the International Space Station.

Robot arm A mechanical arm which is controlled by a computer, in turn programmed to carry out tasks such as picking and moving items.

Rover A vehicle that explores the surface of another planet or moon, controlled by people on Earth.

Sensor A device that detects or measures something.

Space probe An unmanned spacecraft sent away from Earth to explore the solar system.

Space Shuttle A crewed spacecraft that could be launched into space, brought back to Earth, and launched again, many times.

Surgery Treatment of illness or injury by repairing or removing parts of the body.

Weld The process of joining metal parts by heating them until they melt together where they touch.

Index

Top robot pioneers

Karel Capek (1890–1938)

The word *robot* appeared for the first time in 1920. It was used in a play called *R.U.R.* (Rossum's Universal Robots) by the Czech writer, Karel Capek. The word was suggested by his brother, Josef, to describe machine-like slave workers in the play.

George Devol (1912–2011)

This American inventor developed the first industrial robot. After working in industry, developing electronic products for a variety of businesses, he turned his attention to automation. One of his first ideas was a machine for picking things up and moving them from place to place in factories. With the help of another robot pioneer, Joseph Engelberger (1925–2015), this idea became the first industrial robot, called Unimate.

Isaac Asimov (1920–1992)

Asimov was a Russian-American scientist and writer known for his science-fiction stories. One of the most famous ideas in his stories is a set of rules called the Three Laws of Robotics. They are programmed into advanced robots to protect people. They are:

1. A robot must not hurt a human being or, by inaction, allow a human being to be hurt.
2. A robot must obey orders from human beings unless this would break the first law.
3. A robot must protect itself from harm unless this would break the first or second laws.

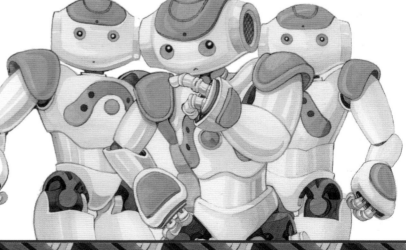

The future of robots

Robots are certain to become more widespread and commonplace in future. As their numbers grow, they will become less expensive and more people will be able to buy them. They are also certain to become smarter and capable of doing more of the jobs done by people today. While some workers may lose their jobs because of this, robots will create new jobs too, because people will be needed to design, build, sell and repair them.

Gastrobots

Today, battery-powered robots have to stop every few hours to recharge their batteries. Some future robots might not need batteries. Instead, they will get the energy they need by eating food and breaking it down inside them as we do. Robots like this, called gastrobots, have already been built and tested in research laboratories.

Did you know?

Robot jockeys race camels in the Middle East! Camel racing is very popular there. The robot jockeys are controlled by radios from cars that drive alongside the racetrack.

In 2014, one of the robots onboard the International Space Station repaired itself by using a second robot. The station's remote manipulator system (RMS) robot arm picked up a second robot, DEXTRE, and used its hands to replace a faulty video camera.

In 2017, a robot was made a citizen of a country for the first time. A humanoid robot called Sophia became a citizen of Saudi Arabia. The robot said she was honoured and proud! Robots like Sophia might be working alongside you in future, or serving you in a shop, or showing you which way to go.